Aa Bb Cc Dd Ee Ff Gg Hh Ii Jj Kk Ll Mm Nn Oo Pp Qq Rr Ss Tt Uu Vv Ww Xx Yy Zz

Let's Learn to Print

Modern Manuscript

by
Sherrill B. Flora

illustrated by
Janet Armbrust

D1451266

Key Education
An imprint of Carson-Dellosa Publishing, LLC
Greensboro, North Carolina

keyeducationpublishing.com

Aa Bb Cc Dd Ee Ff Gg Hh Ii Jj Kk Ll Mm Nn Oo Pp Qq Rr Ss Tt Uu Vv Ww Xx Yy Zz

CONGRATULATIONS ON YOUR PURCHASE OF A KEY EDUCATION PRODUCT!

The editors at Key Education are former teachers who bring experience, enthusiasm, and quality to each and every product. Thousands of teachers have looked to our staff for new and innovative resources to make their work more enjoyable and rewarding. Key Education is committed to developing educational materials that will assist teachers in building a strong and developmentally appropriate curriculum for young children.

PLAN FOR GREAT TEACHING EXPERIENCES WHEN YOU USE EDUCATIONAL MATERIALS FROM KEY EDUCATION PUBLISHING

Key Education

An imprint of Carson-Dellosa Publishing, LLC
PO Box 35665
Greensboro, NC 27425 USA
keyeducationpublishing.com

Credits

Author: Sherrill B. Flora
Illustrations: Janet Armbrust
Editors: Kelly Huxmann, George C. Flora
Cover Design: Mary Claire
Production: Key Education
Cover Photography: © BananaStock

ISBN 1-933052-01-5
01-240128091

Contents

Handwriting Ideas

Learning to print is an exciting experience for a young child. It is important that children learn how to print correctly. Here are some helpful hints that will assist children in learning how to print letters using the correct handwriting strokes.

SAND TRAYS

Take a cookie sheet and cover the bottom with either sand or salt. Have the children practice printing letters in the sand with their fingers. They will be able to feel how each letter is formed.

MOSAIC LETTERS

Gather fifty-two 4" x 6" index cards, glue, uncooked beans, macaroni, or seeds. Make 26 uppercase letters and 26 lowercase letters by drawing one letter on each card. Trace over the letters with glue and then lay the beans, pasta, or seeds on top of the glue. Let dry. When you have finished making the alphabet letters, they can be used for a variety of activities:

- Use as flash cards for letter identification.
- Place the cards in alphabetical order.
- Use the cards to match uppercase letters to lowercase letters.

CLAY OR PLAY DOUGH LETTERS

Prepare a set of alphabet cards ahead of time. Give the children play-dough or clay and teach them how to roll the clay so that it looks like a long worm. Have the children use the clay to form letters that correspond to the alphabet card.

When you first begin this activity, choose some of the easier alphabet letters such as O, C, V, X, L, and T. As the children become more skilled in shaping the letters, try introducing some of the more difficult letters.

GLUE LETTERS

Give each child a set of cards with one alphabet letter printed on each card. Let the children trace over the letters with white glue. Let the glue dry. Have the children use their index fingers to trace over the dried glue letters. This will allow them to feel how each letter is formed and to practice tracing the correct direction of each letter.

Aa Bb Cc Dd Ee Ff Gg Hh Ii Jj Kk Ll Mm Nn Oo Pp Qq Rr Ss Tt Uu Vv Ww Xx Yy Zz

Reference Card for Three-Ring Binder

Uppercase Letters

A B C D E F G H I
J K L M N O P Q R
S T U V W X Y Z

Lowercase Letters

a b c d e f g h i j
k l m n o p q r
s t u v w x y z

Aa Bb Cc Dd Ee Ff Gg Hh Ii Jj Kk Ll Mm Nn Oo Pp Qq Rr Ss Tt Uu Vv Ww Xx Yy Zz

Let's Learn About Guide Lines

This is
the top line. →

This is
the middle
line. →

This is
the bottom
line. →

o j l L F

Try making some big letters. Be sure to touch the lines.

Name _____

Ll

Print your name.

Anders

Look at the laughing lion.

HA! HA! HA!

Color.

Trace the lowercase letters.

l l l l l l l l l l Lion

Print all by yourself.   *Circle your favorite letters.*

l l l l l l l l l l Lion

Circle "l" and "L."

L l l T i L O l t L Y l m

Trace the uppercase letters.

L L L L L L L Look

Print all by yourself.   *Circle your favorite letters.*

L L L L L Look

Circle your favorite letters.

Print your name.

Trace and print.

l l l l l l

Trace and print.

L L L L L L

Trace the sentence.

Leslie likes you.

Print the sentence all by yourself.

Trace the sentence.

Listen to her laugh.

Print the sentence all by yourself.

Print your name.

Ike said, "I like ice cream."

Color.

Trace the lowercase letters.

i i i i i i i i i i i i i i in

Print all by yourself.

Circle your favorite letters.

Circle "i" and "I."

h i I T i v I h J i r I

Trace the uppercase letters.

I I I I I I I I I I I Ice

Print all by yourself.

Circle your favorite letters.

Print your name.

Circle your
favorite letters.

Trace and print.

i i i i i

Trace and print.

I I I I I

Trace the sentence.

I like to print.

Print the sentence all by yourself.

Trace the sentence.

I like Mike and Ike.

Print the sentence all by yourself.

Tt

Print your name.

The tiger has a long tail.   Color.

Trace the lowercase letters.

t t t t t t t tent

Print all by yourself.   Circle your favorite letters.

Circle "T" and "t."

t L T t k h T P t I T s

Trace the uppercase letters.

T T T T T T T Tim

Print all by yourself.   Circle your favorite letters.

Aa Bb Cc Dd Ee Ff Gg Hh Ii Jj Kk Ll Mm Nn Oo Pp Qq Rr Ss Tt Uu Vv Ww Xx Yy Zz

Circle your favorite letters.

Print your name.

Trace and print.

t t t t t

Trace and print.

T T T T T

Trace the sentence.

Tell Tom to listen.

Print the sentence all by yourself.

Trace the sentence.

Tim is too tall.

Print the sentence all by yourself.

O o

Print your name.

The _ow_l _on_ly likes _to_ read.

Color.

Trace the lowercase letters.

o o o o o o o o o o off

Print all by yourself.

Circle your favorite letters.

Circle "O" and "o."

O o Q a O o o S O K o m P

Trace the uppercase letters.

O O O O O O O Owl

Print all by yourself.

Circle your favorite letters.

Print your name.

Circle your
favorite letters.

Trace and print.

O O O O O O

Trace and print.

O O O O O O

Trace the sentence.

Look at the books.

Print the sentence all by yourself.

Trace the sentence.

Look at Otto.

Print the sentence all by yourself.

C c

Print your name.

The cat is eating cake and candy.
Color.

Trace the lowercase letters.

c c c c c c c c c c a t

Print all by yourself.   Circle your favorite letters.

Circle "C" and "c."

c C a o C c O q c a C e

Trace the uppercase letters.

C C C C C C C C a t

Print all by yourself.   Circle your favorite letters.

Print your name.

Circle your favorite letters.

Trace and print.

C C C C C

Trace and print.

C C C C C

Trace the sentence.

Catch the ball, Carl.

Print the sentence all by yourself.

Trace the sentence.

Carol, come here.

Print the sentence all by yourself.

Aa

Print your name.

Ants love to eat apples.

Color.

Trace the lowercase letters.

a a a a a a a ant

Print all by yourself.

Circle your favorite letters.

Circle "A" and "a."

A c a A V a V A X a N

Trace the uppercase letters.

A A A A A A A Ant

Print all by yourself.

Circle your favorite letters.

Circle your favorite letters.

Print your name.

Trace and print.

a a a a a

Trace and print.

A A A A A

Trace the sentence.

Ann is very happy.

Print the sentence all by yourself.

Trace the sentence.

Apples are red.

Print the sentence all by yourself.

Print your name.

D d

Dave the dog likes to dig.

Color.

Trace the lowercase letters.

d d d d d d d dog

Print all by yourself.

Circle your favorite letters.

Circle "D" and "d."

D d b p O D d D b d Q

Trace the uppercase letters.

D D D D D D David

Print all by yourself.

Circle your favorite letters.

Print your name.

Circle your
favorite letters.

Trace and print.

d d d d d

Trace and print.

D D D D D

Trace the sentence.

Did you draw that?

Print the sentence all by yourself.

Trace the sentence.

Ducks like to dive.

Print the sentence all by yourself.

E e

Print your name.

Ellie Elephant is eating eggs.   Color.

Trace the lowercase letters.

e e e e e e e e e e e egg

Print all by yourself.   Circle your favorite letters.

Circle "E" and "e."

e E F c E f e F a E e n

Trace the uppercase letters.

E E E E E E Ellie

Print all by yourself.   Circle your favorite letters.

Circle your favorite letters.

Print your name.

Trace and print.

e e e e e

Trace and print.

E E F F F

Trace the sentence.

Eddie likes eggs.

Print the sentence all by yourself.

Trace the sentence.

Ellie eats beans.

Print the sentence all by yourself.

Ff

Print your name.

Fred the fox is fishing.

Color.

Trace the lowercase letters.

ff ＿＿＿＿＿＿＿＿ fish

Print all by yourself.   Circle your favorite letters.

Circle "F" and "f."

F f j f E e H F h F M f

Trace the uppercase letters.

FF ＿＿＿＿＿＿ Frank

Print all by yourself.   Circle your favorite letters.

Circle your
favorite letters.

Print your name.

Trace and print.

f f f f f

Trace and print.

F F F F F

Trace the sentence.

Find a funny face.

Print the sentence all by yourself.

Trace the sentence.

Fred is a fluffy fox.

Print the sentence all by yourself.

Hh

Print your name.

Color.

Hilda Hippo has a hat.

Trace the lowercase letters.

h h h h h h h hat

Print all by yourself.

Circle your favorite letters.

Circle "H" and "h."

h n H b k H h K h n H d

Trace the uppercase letters.

H H H H H H H Harry

Print all by yourself.

Circle your favorite letters.

Aa Bb Cc Dd Ee Ff Gg Hh Ii Jj Kk Ll Mm Nn Oo Pp Qq Rr Ss Tt Uu Vv Ww Xx Yy Zz

Print your name.

Circle your favorite letters.

Trace and print.

h h h h h

Trace and print.

H H H H H

Trace the sentence.

Hike up the hill.

Print the sentence all by yourself.

Trace the sentence.

Harriet is a hen.

Print the sentence all by yourself.

Gg

Print your name.

The goats are giving gifts.

Color.

Trace the lowercase letters.

g g g g g g g g g goat

Print all by yourself.

Circle your favorite letters.

Circle "G" and "g."

q G P p g G G Q P g C G g q

Trace the uppercase letters.

G G G G G G G G Gg

Print all by yourself.

Circle your favorite letters.

Aa Bb Cc Dd Ee Ff Gg Hh Ii Jj Kk Ll Mm Nn Oo Pp Qq Rr Ss Tt Uu Vv Ww Xx Yy Zz

Circle your favorite letters.

Print your name.

Trace and print.

g g g g g

Trace and print.

G G G G G

Trace the sentence.

Girls like to giggle.

Print the sentence all by yourself.

Trace the sentence.

Gus has a goat.

Print the sentence all by yourself.

Jj

Print your name.

Joe Jaguar jumps rope.

Color.

Trace the lowercase letters.

j j j j j j j j j jump

Print all by yourself.   Circle your favorite letters.

Circle "J" and "j."

q J p j U J P j J q g j

Trace the uppercase letters.

J J J J J J J John

Print all by yourself.   Circle your favorite letters.

Circle your favorite letters.

Print your name.

Trace and print.

j j j j j j

Trace and print.

J J J J J

Trace the sentence.

Jack and Jill jump.

Print the sentence all by yourself.

Trace the sentence.

John flies a jet.

Print the sentence all by yourself.

Q q

Print your name.

The queen makes quilts.

Color.

Trace the lowercase letters.

q q q q q q q quiet

Print all by yourself.   Circle your favorite letters.

Circle "Q" and "q."

q Q P p q D Q O q C Q a

Trace the uppercase letters.

Q Q Q Q Q Q Queen

Print all by yourself.   Circle your favorite letters.

Circle your favorite letters.

Print your name.

Trace and print.

q q q q q

Trace and print.

Q Q Q Q Q

Trace the sentence.

Quack like a duck.

Print the sentence all by yourself.

Trace the sentence.

The queen quilts.

Print the sentence all by yourself.

P p

Print your name.

Color.

Peggy Pig plans to be a pilot.

Trace the lowercase letters.

p p P P P P P P P Pig

Print all by yourself.

Circle your favorite letters.

Circle "P" and "p."

P q p g P d p P B J p b

Trace the uppercase letters.

P P P P P P P P Pink

Print all by yourself.

Circle your favorite letters.

33

Let's Learn to Print: Modern Manuscript

Circle your favorite letters.

Print your name.

Trace and print.

p p p p p p

Trace and print.

P P P P P P

Trace the sentence.

Pablo has a pet pig.

Print the sentence all by yourself.

Trace the sentence.

Pandas are pretty.

Print the sentence all by yourself.

Uu

Print your name.

The _unicorn_ has an _u_mbrella.

Color.

Trace the lowercase letters.

U U u u u u under

Print all by yourself.

Circle your favorite letters.

Circle "U" and "u."

N u b h U D u U b u n U

Trace the uppercase letters.

U U U U U U Up

Print all by yourself.

Circle your favorite letters.

Aa Bb Cc Dd Ee Ff Gg Hh Ii Jj Kk Ll Mm Nn Oo Pp Qq Rr Ss Tt Uu Vv Ww Xx Yy Zz

Circle your favorite letters.

Print your name.

Trace and print.

U U u u u

Trace and print.

U U u u u

Trace the sentence.

Use our umbrella.

Print the sentence all by yourself.

Trace the sentence.

Unicorns are cute.

Print the sentence all by yourself.

S s

Print your name.

Sara Seal sits in the sun.

Color.

Trace the lowercase letters.

s s s s s s s s s s s sit

Print all by yourself.

Circle your favorite letters.

Circle "S" and "s."

X S s C S e K S u s E s

Trace the uppercase letters.

S S S S S S Sam

Print all by yourself.

Circle your favorite letters.

Circle your favorite letters.

Print your name.

Trace and print.

S S s s s

Trace and print.

S S S S S

Trace the sentence.

Sue sings songs.

Print the sentence all by yourself.

Trace the sentence.

Seals slip and slide.

Print the sentence all by yourself.

B b

Print your name.

Baby Bear
blows bubbles.

Color.

Trace the lowercase letters.

b b b b b b b ball

Print all by yourself.   Circle your favorite letters.

Circle "B" and "b."

b d p B D B d b B d P b

Trace the uppercase letters.

B B B B B B B Ben

Print all by yourself.   Circle your favorite letters.

Print your name.

Circle your favorite letters.

Trace and print.

b b b b b

Trace and print.

B B B B B

Trace the sentence.

Bob likes baseball.

Print the sentence all by yourself.

Trace the sentence.

Give baby a bottle.

Print the sentence all by yourself.

R r

Print your name.

Robert Rabbit runs the race.

Color.

Trace the lowercase letters.

r r r r r r r r r r run

Print all by yourself.

Circle your favorite letters.

Circle "R" and "r."

r P R R r n u R B h R H r

Trace the uppercase letters.

R R R R R R Robin

Print all by yourself.

Circle your favorite letters.

Circle your favorite letters.

Print your name.

Trace and print.

r r r r r

Trace and print.

R R R R R

Trace the sentence.

Ride in the rocket.

Print the sentence all by yourself.

Trace the sentence.

Rock and roll!

Print the sentence all by yourself.

Aa Bb Cc Dd Ee Ff Gg Hh Ii Jj Kk Ll Mm Nn Oo Pp Qq Rr Ss Tt Uu Vv Ww Xx Yy Zz

Nn

Print your name.

Ned Newt reads
the newspaper.

Color.

Trace the lowercase letters.

n n n n n n n nest

Print all by yourself.

Circle your favorite letters.

Circle "N" and "n."

n N M n b n N V W m h N

Trace the uppercase letters.

N N N N N N Nick

Print all by yourself.

Circle your favorite letters.

Aa Bb Cc Dd Ee Ff Gg Hh Ii Jj Kk Ll Mm Nn Oo Pp Qq Rr Ss Tt Uu Vv Ww Xx Yy Zz

Circle your favorite letters.

Print your name.

Trace and print.

n n n n n

Trace and print.

N N N N N

Trace the sentence.

Ned is so nice.

Print the sentence all by yourself.

Trace the sentence.

Nan is never late.

Print the sentence all by yourself.

Print your name.

Many monkeys make music.   Color.

Trace the lowercase letters.

m m m m m m m mine

Print all by yourself.

Circle your favorite letters.

Circle "M" and "m."

M m N m H M u u M W m u

Trace the uppercase letters.

M M M M M M M Mike

Print all by yourself.

Circle your favorite letters.

Aa Bb Cc Dd Ee Ff Gg Hh Ii Jj Kk Ll Mm Nn Oo Pp Qq Rr Ss Tt Uu Vv Ww Xx Yy Zz

Circle your favorite letters.

Print your name.

Trace and print.

m m m m m m

Trace and print.

M M M M M M

Trace the sentence.

Man on the moon.

Print the sentence all by yourself.

Trace the sentence.

Martin is a mouse.

Print the sentence all by yourself.

Print your name.

Violet Vulture
plays the violin.

Color.

Trace the lowercase letters.

V V v v v v v v v v v vase

Print all by yourself.

Circle your favorite letters.

Circle "V" and "v."

v V x V U w v W N V x v

Trace the uppercase letters.

V V V V V V V Vern

Print all by yourself.

Circle your favorite letters.

*Circle your
favorite letters.*

Print your name.

Trace and print.

V V v v v v

Trace and print.

V V V V V V

Trace the sentence.

Violets are lovely.

Print the sentence all by yourself.

Trace the sentence.

Vultures are big.

Print the sentence all by yourself.

Print your name.

Color.

Yani Yak loves
his yellow yo-yo.

Trace the lowercase letters.

y y y y y y y y yake

Print all by yourself.

Circle your favorite letters.

Circle "Y" and "y."

y x p g V V Y j j Y y X y Y

Trace the uppercase letters.

Y Y Y Y Y Y Y Y Yak

Print all by yourself.

Circle your favorite letters.

Circle your favorite letters.

Print your name.

Trace and print.

y y y y y

Trace and print.

Y Y Y Y Y

Trace the sentence.

The yak is yawning.

Print the sentence all by yourself.

Trace the sentence.

Yogurt is yummy.

Print the sentence all by yourself.

Print your name.

Wally Walrus swims in the water. Color.

Trace the lowercase letters.

w w w w w w water

Print all by yourself.

Circle your favorite letters.

Circle "W" and "w."

W w m w v W U V w W X V

Trace the uppercase letters.

W W W W W W W W

Print all by yourself.

Circle your favorite letters.

Print your name.

Circle your favorite letters.

Trace and print.

W W w w w

Trace and print.

W W W W W

Trace the sentence.

Wash the windows.

Print the sentence all by yourself.

Trace the sentence.

Worms wiggle.

Print the sentence all by yourself.

Print your name.

Color.

Xavier plays the xylophone.

Trace the lowercase letters.

X X x x x x x x x box

Print all by yourself.

Circle your favorite letters.

Circle "X" and "x."

x y v X W v V X x Y x X

Trace the uppercase letters.

X X X X X X X-ray

Print all by yourself.

Circle your favorite letters.

Print your name.

Circle your
favorite letters.

Trace and print.

X X x x x

Trace and print.

X X x x x

Trace the sentence.

X-ray the box.

Print the sentence all by yourself.

Trace the sentence.

The fox is furry.

Print the sentence all by yourself.

Aa Bb Cc Dd Ee Ff Gg Hh Ii Jj Kk Ll Mm Nn Oo Pp Qq Rr Ss Tt Uu Vv Ww Xx Yy Zz

K k

Print your name.

Kelly Kangaroo flies a kite.

Color.

Trace the lowercase letters.

k k k k k k k k kite

Print all by yourself.

Circle your favorite letters.

Circle "K" and "k."

K k X v X K K k T K k F

Trace the uppercase letters.

K K K K K K Katie

Print all by yourself.

Circle your favorite letters.

*Circle your
favorite letters.*

Print your name.

Trace and print.

k k k k k

Trace and print.

K K K K K

Trace the sentence.

The koala is kooky.

Print the sentence all by yourself.

Trace the sentence.

Keshia is very kind.

Print the sentence all by yourself.

Z z

Print your name.

Zack Zebra zips his zipper.

Color.

Trace the lowercase letters.

z z z z z z z z z z z z zoo

Print all by yourself.

Circle your favorite letters.

Circle "Z" and "z."

Z z z A Z z H v L Z S s z

Trace the uppercase letters.

Z Z Z Z Z Z Z Z Zelda

Print all by yourself.

Circle your favorite letters.

Print your name.

Circle your favorite letters.

Trace and print.

z z z z z

Trace and print.

Z Z Z Z Z

Trace the sentence.

Zebras have stripes.

Print the sentence all by yourself.

Trace the sentence.

Ziggy ran zigzag.

Print the sentence all by yourself.

Review
Lowercase Letters

Print your name.

Trace.

a b c d e f g h

i j k l m n o p q

r s t u v w x y z

Print your own lowercase alphabet.

Review
Uppercase Letters

Print your name.

Trace.

A B C D E F G H I

J K L M N O P Q R

S T U V W X Y Z

Print your own uppercase alphabet.

Aa Bb Cc Dd Ee Ff Gg Hh Ii Jj Kk Ll Mm Nn Oo Pp Qq Rr Ss Tt Uu Vv Ww Xx Yy Zz

FINAL
ASSESSMENT

Print your name.

Print your own lowercase alphabet.

Print your own uppercase alphabet.

Aa Bb Cc Dd Ee Ff Gg Hh Ii Jj Kk Ll Mm Nn Oo Pp Qq Rr Ss Tt Uu Vv Ww Xx Yy Zz